HUMPHREY GOES TO THE BALL

CHRIS RIDDELL

GRAFTON BOOKS

A Division of the Collins Publishing Group

LONDON GLASGOW
TORONTO SYDNEY AUCKLAND

'Wake up, Humphrey!' cried Bird excitedly. 'We've got a letter.'

Humphrey gave a big yawn and opened one eye.

'Well, aren't you going to open it, Bird?' he asked.

Bird opened the envelope. Inside was an invitation to the Mayor's Fancy Dress Ball.

'But what can I wear?' Humphrey puzzled.

'You could keep that bath hat on and go as Little Miss Muffet, and I could be the spider beside you,' said Bird.

'But I'm not little,' said Humphrey sadly.

Then Humphrey had an idea. 'I can go as a pirate,' he said, 'and you can be my parrot.'

They cut out a pirate's hat, some ear-rings and an eyepatch for Humphrey, and found a feather duster to make a parrot's tail for Bird.

Soon they were ready to go. Humphrey used a broom as a crutch and swung his cardboard cutlass about. Bird sat on his shoulder and practised saying 'pieces of eight, pieces of eight' (which is what pirates' parrots say in real life).

'Ahoy there, me hearties!' called Humphrey
as they sailed into town on their motorbike.

At the Fancy Dress Ball there were people dressed as kings and queens, doctors and dames, clowns and cowgirls. But Humphrey was the only pirate with a parrot.

'Welcome,' said the Mayor, shaking Humphrey's hand.

'Pieces of eight,' squawked Bird.

Then the band began to play.

Humphrey danced with a cowgirl, but she kept tripping over his broom.

Then Bird said, 'Look! There's a hippo over there.'

'I'll ask her to dance,' said Humphrey excitedly.

He rushed over and grabbed the hippo by the hand, and they began to dance.

Humphrey was good at rock 'n' roll dancing, and everyone gathered around to watch.

At the end of the dance, Humphrey threw his partner up in the air – wheeee! But then she came down – wheeee! – and he dropped her.

'Butterfingers,' said Bird.

'Oh no!' said Humphrey. 'Her head's come off.'

There on the floor was the Mayor, with the head of his hippo fancy dress costume beside him.

'I'm so sorry,' said Humphrey.

'No harm done,' laughed the Mayor, 'but I want you to do something for me.'

'What's that?' asked Humphrey.

'Take some dancing lessons before next year's Ball!' said the Mayor.

'Pieces of eight!' said Bird.

For Francie

Grafton Books
A Division of the Collins Publishing Group
8 Grafton Street, London W1X 3LA

Published by Grafton Books 1986
Copyright © Chris Riddell 1986

British Library Cataloguing in Publication Data
Riddell, Chris
    Humphrey goes to the ball.
    I. Title
    823'.914[J]   PZ7

ISBN 0–246–12966–2

Printed in Belgium by
Henri Proost

PRINTED IN BELGIUM BY

proost

INTERNATIONAL BOOK PRODUCTION